READING POWER

Sammy Sosa

Home Run Hitter

Rob Kirkpatrick

The Rosen Publishing Group's
PowerKids Press ™
New York

1

For my father.

Published in 2000 by The Rosen Publishing Group, Inc.
29 East 21st Street, New York, NY 10010

First Edition

Book design: Michael de Guzman

Photo Credits: p. 5 © Jonathan Daniel/Allsport; p. 7 © Michael Zito/SportsChrome USA; p. 9 © Steve Woltman/SportsChrome; p. 11 © Reuters/Adrees A. Latif/Archive Photos; p. 13 © Janice E. Rettaliata/Allsport; pp. 15, 22 Vincent Laforet/Allsport; p. 17,19 © Rob Tringali Jr./SportsChrome; p. 21 © Sporting News/Archive Photos

Text Consultant: Linda J. Kirkpatrick, Reading Specialist/Reading Recovery Teacher

Kirkpatrick, Rob.
    Sammy Sosa: home-run hitter / by Rob Kirkpatrick.
    p. cm. — (Reading power)
    Includes index.
    Summary: Introduces the home-run hitting fielder for the Chicago Cubs,
Sammy Sosa.
    ISBN 0-8239-5534-6
    1. Sosa, Sammy, 1968– Juvenile literature. 2. Baseball players—Dominican
Republic Biography Juvenile literature. [1. Sosa, Sammy, 1968– 2. Baseball
players.] I. Title. II. Series.
    GV865.S59 K57 1999
    796.357'092—dc21
    [B]   99-16000
                                        CIP

Manufactured in the United States of America

Contents

Sammy Sosa plays baseball. He is on the Chicago Cubs.

5

Sammy plays in the outfield. He uses his glove to get fly balls.

Sammy is number 21 on the Cubs.

Sammy is happy when his team wins. He gives "high fives" when his team wins.

ALEXANDER
24

CHICAGO
21

11

Sammy played for the Chicago White Sox. He liked to bat for the White Sox.

13

Mark McGwire is friends with Sammy. Mark plays for the St. Louis Cardinals.

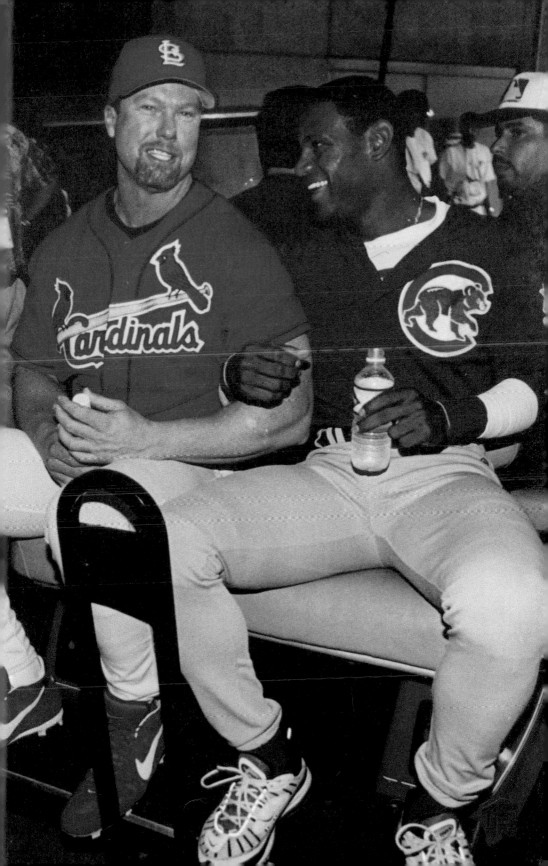

Sammy hits a lot of home runs. Sammy hit 66 home runs in 1998.

17

Sammy likes to hit the ball.
He can hit it way up in
the air.

19

People like Sammy's smile.
He makes people happy.

21

The Sosa family loves
Sammy. He likes it when
they see his games.

Here are more books to read about Sammy Sosa:

Sammy Sosa
by Richard Brenner
William Morrow & Company (1999)

Sammy Sosa
by Laura Driscoll, illustrated by
Ken Call
Grosset & Dunlap (1999)

To learn more about baseball, check out this Web site:

http://CNNSI.com/

Glossary

bat (BAT) When a player stands by home plate and tries to hit the ball.

fly ball (FLY BAWL) A ball that a batter has hit way up in the air.

home run (HOHM RUHN) When a batter hits the ball out of the park and gets to run around the bases.

outfield (OWT-feeld) Part of a baseball field where right fielder, center fielder, and left fielder play.

Index

Word Count: 123

Note to Librarians, Teachers, and Parents

If reading is a challenge, Reading Power is a solution! Reading Power is perfect for readers who want high-interest subject matter at an accessible reading level. These fact-filled, photo-illustrated books are designed for readers who want straightforward vocabulary, engaging topics, and a manageable reading experience. With clear picture/text correspondence, leveled Reading Power books put the reader in charge. Now readers have the power to get the information they want and the skills they need in a user-friendly format.